AF221000

NEW YORK
YANKEES

BY ANTHONY K. HEWSON

SportsZone

An Imprint of Abdo Publishing
abdobooks.com

abdobooks.com

Published by Abdo Publishing, a division of ABDO, PO Box 398166, Minneapolis, Minnesota 55439. Copyright © 2023 by Abdo Consulting Group, Inc. International copyrights reserved in all countries. No part of this book may be reproduced in any form without written permission from the publisher. SportsZone™ is a trademark and logo of Abdo Publishing.

Printed in China.
102022
012023

Editor: Steph Giedd
Series Designer: Becky Daum

Library of Congress Control Number: 2022940487

Publisher's Cataloging-in-Publication Data

Names: Hewson, Anthony K., author.
Title: New York Yankees / by Anthony K. Hewson
Description: Minneapolis, Minnesota: Abdo Publishing, 2023 | Series: Inside MLB | Includes online resources and index.
Identifiers: ISBN 9781098290269 (lib. bdg.) | ISBN 9781098275464 (ebook)
Subjects: LCSH: New York Yankees (Baseball team)--Juvenile literature. | Baseball teams--Juvenile literature. | Professional sports--Juvenile literature. | Sports franchises--Juvenile literature. | Major League Baseball (Organization)--Juvenile literature.
Classification: DDC 796.35764--dc23

CONTENTS

CHAPTER 1

THE HOUSE THAT RUTH BUILT 4

CHAPTER 2

LEGACY OF LEGENDS 12

CHAPTER 3

THE PRIDE OF THE YANKEES 20

CHAPTER 4

A MODERN DYNASTY 30

TIMELINE 42
TEAM FACTS 44
TEAM TRIVIA 45
GLOSSARY 46
MORE INFORMATION 47
ONLINE RESOURCES 47
INDEX 48
ABOUT THE AUTHOR 48

THE HOUSE THAT RUTH BUILT

Derek Jeter slowly walked to the plate as the fans at Yankee Stadium rose and applauded. A familiar chant of "DE-rek JEE-ter" rose from the crowd. For 20 years, Jeter had given Yankees fans thrills in one of baseball's most famous ballparks. Now, the 40-year-old was coming to bat at Yankee Stadium for the final time.

It was fitting that it would come in a pressure spot. Over the course of his career, Jeter had earned the nickname "Captain Clutch" for his record-setting playoff performances. Now, in the bottom of the ninth inning, Jeter came up with a runner on second base and one out. It was September 25, 2014, the final

Derek Jeter celebrates after his final hit in Yankee Stadium on September 25, 2014.

Hall of Fame shortstop Jeter spent his entire 20-year career with the Yankees.

home game of the regular season. Jeter had a chance to send himself out a walk-off winner.

Baltimore Orioles righty Evan Meek took the sign from his catcher, then delivered the pitch. There are 49,642 seats at Yankee Stadium, but none of them were being used. The standing crowd watched as Jeter went after the first-pitch changeup. As he had done so many times before, he shot the ball through the hole between first and second.

Antoan Richardson was the Yankees' runner on second base. He sprinted around third and headed for home. The throw from right field bounced in and out of catcher Caleb Joseph's glove as Richardson dove across home plate for the winning run. Rounding first, Jeter threw both arms in the air. As the stadium erupted, teammates mobbed the shortstop. After the on-field celebration was over, Jeter walked to the dugout. There, former teammates Bernie Williams, Andy Pettitte, Mariano Rivera, Tino Martinez, and Jorge Posada were waiting for him. Jeter hugged them all, then walked off the Yankee Stadium field for the final time.

THE HIGHLANDERS

Jeter had the honor of playing in two legendary ballparks, both called Yankee Stadium. Each park has seen some of the best baseball players ever to call it home. The new version of the famous Bronx, New York, stadium was completed in 2009. It replaced the original park, which had opened in 1923. Before that, New York's American League (AL) baseball team played in stadiums called Hilltop Park and then Polo Grounds. And the team was not yet called the Yankees.

The AL began play in 1901, but it had no team in New York. That changed two years later when a failing Baltimore team folded. New York was then granted a new franchise to

Hall of Fame pitcher Jack Chesbro poses in his Highlanders uniform during his first season with New York in 1903.

replace Baltimore, so two businessmen started a team in the United States' largest city. Because they played at one of the most elevated spots on the island of Manhattan, the team quickly earned the nickname "Highlanders."

The Highlanders were successful right away. In their second season, they won 92 games. The star of the team was pitcher Jack Chesbro. The righty started 51 games and completed 48 of them. When the season was over, he had won 41 games, a modern AL record that still stands.

However, on the final day of the season, the Highlanders needed to win both games of a doubleheader against the Boston Americans, who later became the Red Sox, to win the AL. In the ninth inning of the first game a wild pitch from Chesbro cost New York the game. It was the first late-season showdown between the two rivals. But it was far from the last.

THE BAMBINO

The Highlanders became the Yankees in 1913 when they moved from Hilltop Park to the Polo Grounds. But through 1919, the team still had not won a league title. After that season, one move would change both teams forever.

Boston had remained an AL power after beating the Highlanders in 1904. However, owner Harry Frazee made a habit of selling his star players' contracts when he needed money. In January 1920, the time had come for him to get rid of outfielder Babe Ruth. The Yankees snatched up "the Bambino" for $100,000.

At the time, baseball was changing. For the previous two decades, home runs were rare. But by 1920, Major League Baseball (MLB) made several rule changes. One of them was to wind baseballs tighter, which made them come off the bat harder and sail farther. Suddenly, the home run was a much bigger part of the game. That was perfect for Ruth, who packed

THE LOOK OF LEGENDS

The Yankees weren't the first team to wear pinstripe uniforms. But they have made the look famous over the years. The team first wore them in 1912 when they were still the Highlanders. They then took the stipes off for the next two seasons. When Colonel Jacob Ruppert bought the team in 1915, he brought the look back, and it has been part of New York's home uniforms ever since.

Hall of Fame slugger Babe Ruth led the majors in several offensive categories including runs, home runs, and runs batted in (RBIs) for many of his 15 seasons in New York.

more punch than anyone in the game. In 1921, just his second season as a Yankee, Ruth broke the all-time home run record by hitting the 139th of his career. And he was just getting started.

Ruth hit 59 home runs in 1921. That broke his record of 54 homers from the previous season. It was his fourth straight season leading the league in homers. He also slugged New York into the World Series for the first time. The Yankees lost a best-of-nine series to the New York Giants of the National League (NL). The rivalry between the teams was intense, as they shared the Polo Grounds as a stadium.

A year later, Yankees owner Colonel Jacob Ruppert began building his own ballpark in the Bronx, which is another area of New York City. It was set to open in 1923. The Giants beat the Yankees in the 1922 World Series again before the Yankees moved out of the Polo Grounds forever.

Yankee Stadium I was built in 1923 for $2.5 million. When it was renovated in 1976, the upgrades cost $160 million.

Yankee Stadium opened on April 18, 1923. Ruth hit a three-run homer in the bottom of the third inning as New York beat Boston 4–1. It was a fitting start for the ballpark that would come to be known as "the House That Ruth Built."

Ruth went on to hit 40 more home runs in 1923. Then he slugged three more in the World Series as the Yankees finally bested the Giants for their first-ever title. Ruth had already hit 238 regular-season home runs when 1923 closed. And he was still only 28 years old.

CHAPTER 2

LEGACY OF LEGENDS

By the time Babe Ruth led the Yankees to their first title in 1923, he was widely regarded as baseball's best-ever player. He was also its most popular player. Everyone wanted to be like the extravagant star. But his huge personality and wild lifestyle weren't always good things.

Ruth ate and drank too much, and he frequently got himself out of shape. It bothered his manager, Miller Huggins, who battled with his star often. Ruth's off-field behavior nearly caught up with him in the mid-1920s. In 1925 he spent time in the hospital with a mystery stomach ailment. It was so bad that some newspapers reported Ruth had died. After six weeks, he returned to the team, but his presence couldn't turn

Babe Ruth earned many nicknames because of his strong bat, including "the Bambino," "the Sultan of Swat," and "the Colossus of Clout."

Hall of Famer Lou Gehrig won the Triple Crown in 1934 after hitting .363 with 49 home runs and 166 RBIs.

around the Yankees' poor season, as they won only 69 games.

MURDERERS' ROW

Ruth was far from New York's only great player. Third baseman Joe Dugan and left fielder Bob Meusel were also dangerous offensive weapons. In 1925 a new legend emerged. First baseman Lou Gehrig started the season as a backup to Wally Pipp. On June 1, Pipp came out of a game due to a headache. Gehrig subbed in and then started the next day. The 22-year-old got three hits. No one knew it at the time, but it was the start of a record streak. Gehrig didn't miss a single game for the next 14 years.

With Gehrig's star rising and a refocused Ruth, the Yankees were back in 1927. Gehrig hit 47 home runs. But Ruth stole the show by breaking his own record and finishing with 60. The rest of the Yankees rounded out one of baseball's most celebrated lineups. With Meusel, Dugan, center fielder Earle

Combs, and second baseman Tony Lazzeri, the Yankees
won 110 games. The batting order earned the nickname
"Murderers' Row."

New York crushed the Pittsburgh Pirates in the World Series
in a four-game sweep. Murderers' Row came back again in
1928 and won 104 games on its way to sweeping the St. Louis
Cardinals for another title. By then there was no doubt which
was the best team in the major leagues.

THE CALLED SHOT

In 1932 Ruth was 37 years old. But he was still a great power
hitter. That year he hit 41 homers. It wasn't enough to lead the
league, as he had the six previous seasons. But it was enough
to get New York back to the World Series for the first time
since 1928.

The Yankees' opponent in 1932 was the Chicago Cubs. New
York won the first two games at home, and then the teams
ventured to Chicago for Game 3. There the Yankees were met
by a hostile crowd. It got even worse after Ruth hit a home run
in the first inning. When he came up again in the fifth, both the
fans and the Cubs' players were heckling the Yankees' star. Ruth
responded by pointing somewhere on the field. Many who
were there, including Gehrig, insisted that Ruth was pointing to
the center-field fence, meaning the slugger intended to hit the

Ruth looks on as his uniform number is retired at Yankee Stadium in 1948.

next pitch over it. Others said Ruth was simply pointing to the Chicago dugout.

No one disputed what happened next. Ruth clobbered a pitch for one of the longest home runs in the history of Chicago's Wrigley Field. The memorable home run became known as "the Called Shot." Whether Ruth predicted the home run is still unknown. But it was the signature moment of a Yankees sweep.

THE LUCKIEST MAN

By 1935 Ruth was slowing down. He wanted to manage the Yankees, but the team didn't agree. Even though he was still productive, Ruth was let go. He had 708 career home runs. The final six came that season, playing for the National League's (NL's) Boston Braves.

The Yankees kept rolling along. Gehrig, still playing every day, was now the team's top star. Starters Red Ruffing and Lefty Gomez were an excellent one-two punch on the mound. And in 1936, the next Yankees legend arrived in New York.

Even though he was just 21 years old, Joe DiMaggio was one of MLB's best players from day one. Nearly half of his 206 hits that season went for extra bases. He filled Ruth's role, but he was Ruth's exact opposite. Ruth was loud and boisterous. DiMaggio was quiet and dignified. Teammates who played with him marveled at how easily he did things. "He never did anything wrong on the field," said teammate Yogi Berra. "I'd never seen him dive for a ball; everything was a chest-high catch."

DiMaggio and Gehrig took the Yankees dynasty to the next level. The team won the World Series every year from 1936 to 1939. During that stretch, they lost only three World Series games.

However, by the time the Yankees swept the Cincinnati Reds in the 1939 World Series, Gehrig wasn't there. He started the season with the team, but he hit just 4-for-28 in eight games before he took himself out of the lineup. He had played in 2,130

Lou Gehrig addresses his team and Yankees fans for the final time in a farewell speech at Yankee Stadium on July 4, 1939.

straight games but would never play again.

Gehrig was feeling ill, but he didn't know why. He visited the famous Mayo Clinic in Rochester, Minnesota. There he was diagnosed with amyotrophic lateral sclerosis. The disease affects the brain's ability to communicate with the body's muscles.

On July 4, 1939, Gehrig spoke to the Yankee Stadium crowd. By now the whole country knew this popular star was battling an incurable disease. Gehrig finally spoke to the crowd and famously said, "For the past two weeks you've been reading about a bad break. Yet today I consider myself the luckiest man on the face of the Earth."

JOLTIN' JOE

Gehrig died less than two years later, on June 2, 1941, of what is now frequently called Lou Gehrig's Disease. The day he passed,

DiMaggio went 2-for-4 against the Cleveland Indians. It was the 19th straight game in which the star center fielder had picked up at least one hit. The New York newspapers had started to take notice of his streak. Before long it would be national news.

On June 17 he reached 30 games to set a new Yankees record. Next up was the modern MLB record of 41 games set in 1922. "Joltin' Joe" tied that on June 29 during the first game of a doubleheader against the Washington Senators. But before the second game, he noticed the bat he had been using was missing. He was upset over the stolen bat. However, he still got a hit in his 42nd straight game while using a new bat, breaking the record.

DiMaggio's amazing display captivated the country. Finally, on July 17 in Cleveland, the run ended. Despite two hard-hit balls, he went 0-for-4. The streak lasted 56 games. For the rest of the 20th century, no one else had a streak longer than 44. And that fall, the Yankees won the World Series again.

61 GAMES

While Joe DiMaggio's 1941 hitting streak was impressive, it wasn't even the longest of his professional career. Playing for the San Francisco Seals in the minor leagues in 1933, DiMaggio had a hitting streak of 61 games.

CHAPTER 3

THE PRIDE OF THE YANKEES

Just two months after the Yankees' 1941 championship, the United States was thrust into World War II (1939–45). Baseball was disrupted as several stars went overseas to help the war effort. Joe DiMaggio was one of them. He missed three seasons from 1943 to 1945. Even without him, the Yankees managed to take home another title in 1943.

DiMaggio returned in 1946 and hit 25 home runs, showing no rust from his time away. The Yankees finished third that season but would soon start the franchise's best title run. DiMaggio was the AL Most Valuable Player (MVP) for the third time in 1947. He hit .315 with 20 homers and 97 RBIs. That fall,

Hall of Famer Joe DiMaggio was the AL MVP three times in his 13 seasons with the Yankees.

he hit two World Series home runs as the Yankees beat the Brooklyn Dodgers 4–3.

Two years later, the Yankees were back in the World Series, once again facing the Dodgers. In five close games, the Yankees beat their city rivals 4–1. It was the start of the greatest championship run in baseball history.

The Yankees repeated in each of the next four years. That passed their own run of four championships from 1936 to 1939. The Yankees swept the Philadelphia Phillies in 1950 and then beat the New York Giants in 1951. In both 1952 and 1953, the Yankees topped the Dodgers again.

HENRICH'S HOMER

Game 1 of the 1949 World Series was tied 0–0 heading into the bottom of the ninth inning at Yankee Stadium. Yankees starter Allie Reynolds and Brooklyn Dodgers ace Don Newcombe had both gone the distance. But Yankees first baseman Tommy Henrich led off the bottom half with a game-winning homer to right field. It was the first walk-off home run in World Series history.

LEGENDARY LINEUPS

The Yankees had always had great stars. And the teams of the 1940s and 1950s were loaded. They had solid hitters like outfielder Hank Bauer and scrappy infielders like shortstop Phil Rizzuto and second baseman Billy Martin.

Shortstop Phil "Scooter" Rizzuto looks to turn a double play in a 1947 game against the Boston Red Sox.

The Yankees' solid lineup helped overcome the loss of DiMaggio, who walked away after the 1951 championship. Injuries had taken their toll on one of the greatest players ever.

However, a new generation of superstars was ready to take his place. Pitcher Whitey Ford joined the Yankees in 1950. He then missed the next two seasons due to military service. But "the Chairman of the Board" returned in 1953. Over the next 15 seasons, he led the AL in wins three times and earned-run average (ERA) twice.

Yogi Berra spent 18 years with the Yankees as a player, and he later managed the team for three seasons.

Yogi Berra joined the team in 1946 as a catcher and later played outfield. He was short and squat and didn't look graceful. But he was a natural player. Berra won three MVP Awards between 1949 and 1955. He was also known for his off-the-wall quotes, such as "Baseball is 90 percent mental. The other half is physical," or "It ain't the heat, it's the humility."

So many strange sayings were attributed to Berra that he told someone later in life that "I never said half the things I said."

The only Yankee who could out-quote Berra was Casey Stengel, the team's brilliant manager. Stengel had already led other teams by the time he joined the Yankees in 1949. He immediately knew he was on to a good thing. "There is less wrong with this team than any I've ever managed," he said. Stengel was right. He left the Yankees after the 1960 season having reached 10 World Series and won seven.

THE MICK

New York's greatest player was the one who took over for DiMaggio in center field. Mickey Mantle, a switch-hitting power hitter, arrived during the 1951 season. After some initial struggles, he quickly became one of the most feared batters in the game. Over the next 18 seasons he led the AL in homers four times, and many of them were towering shots. The laid-back country boy from Oklahoma also had good looks and charm. He was the idol of nearly every Yankees baseball fan for nearly two decades.

Mickey Mantle won the AL Triple Crown in 1956 after leading the league with a .353 batting average, 52 home runs, and 130 RBIs.

The only thing that held Mantle back was his own body. "The Mick" battled constant leg pain that often kept him out of the lineup. Through it all he still hit 536 career home runs and won three MVP Awards. After his career ended in 1968, many wondered what he could have accomplished if he hadn't missed so many games.

PERFECTION

The Yankees entered the 1956 World Series loaded with Berra, Ford, Mantle, Bauer, and All-Star infielder and catcher Elston Howard anchoring the lineup. But it was a little-known pitcher who stole the show in the World Series.

Don Larsen went 11–5 as a part-time starter in 1956. No one was expecting greatness when he took the mound for the pivotal Game 5 of the World Series against the Dodgers. In Game 2 he had been roughed up in a 13–8 loss. Larsen didn't even know he would pitch Game 5 until he showed up to Yankee Stadium. But he started off well, striking out four of the first nine men he faced. In the fifth inning he got some defensive help as Mantle made a great running catch in left-center field.

From there Larsen was in total control as New York built a 2–0 lead. Entering the ninth inning, he had six strikeouts and had retired all 24 batters. After two quick outs, the final batter was pinch-hitter Dale Mitchell. Larsen struck him out on a 1–2 pitch. Berra raced out and jumped into Larsen's arms to celebrate the first perfect game in World Series history.

Don Larsen delivers a pitch during his perfect-game performance in Game 5 of the 1956 World Series.

The unlikely hero's feat was the only MLB postseason no-hitter until 2010.

THE CHASE

In 1961 baseball expanded its schedule from 154 to 162 games. Home runs were also on the rise throughout the league. Many wondered before the season if someone could break Babe Ruth's record of 60 set in 1927.

Roger Maris hits his 61st homer to break Babe Ruth's single-season record on October 1, 1961.

Most people thought Mantle would be the one to do it. But the team also had right fielder Roger Maris, who had joined the Yankees in 1960 and won that year's MVP Award. To everyone's surprise, he was also hitting homers at a record pace in 1961. As both players continued their strong seasons, the media pressure intensified. Mantle had been in the bright New York spotlight for 11 seasons and was used to it. The quiet, private Maris was not. And with Maris having been with the Yankees for only a short time, many fans and reporters let him know they hoped Mantle would break the record, not him. He was told that he "wasn't a true Yankee" by fans and even started receiving death threats.

The strain of the season caused Maris's hair to fall out. But he kept hitting. Eventually, a hip infection took Mantle out of the race in September. Maris marched on and hit his 61st homer on the last day of the season against the Boston Red Sox. He added one more in the World Series as the Yankees beat the Cincinnati Reds 4–1.

Together, Maris and Mantle were known as "the M & M Boys." The pair led the Yankees back to the World Series in 1962. New York won a thrilling seven-game series over the San Francisco Giants, who had moved out of New York five years earlier.

It was New York's 10th championship in the last 16 seasons and 20th overall. But little did Yankees fans know it would be the team's last for more than a decade. The Yankees went to the World Series in 1963 and 1964 but lost both years. By the 1969 season Berra, Ford, Maris, and Mantle were all gone. It was the end of the greatest dynasty the major leagues have ever seen.

A MODERN DYNASTY

Starting in 1965, the Yankees had three losing seasons in a row. That had not happened since 1913 to 1915. And New York's postseason drought stretched into the mid-1970s. The team's biggest news came off the field. Successful shipping businessman George Steinbrenner bought the Yankees in 1973. He quickly became one of baseball's most controversial owners.

Steinbrenner was used to getting his way, and he brought an impatient attitude to ownership. He was quick to get rid of underperforming players and even quicker to fire his managers. Between 1975 and 1990, Steinbrenner went through more than one manager in a season nine times. One of his favorite targets was Billy Martin. Steinbrenner hired and fired Martin five times.

Yankees manager George Steinbrenner, *top right*, poses with manager Billy Martin, *top left*, catcher Thurman Munson, *bottom left*, and outfielder Reggie Jackson, *bottom right*, in 1980.

In 1974 free agency came to baseball. It was perfect for an owner like Steinbrenner. He could go out and buy stars instead of waiting for prospects to develop. By 1976 he had brought in star pitcher Catfish Hunter and traded for first baseman Chris Chambliss. That complemented homegrown talent like catcher Thurman Munson and second baseman Willie Randolph, who was brought in from a trade with the Pittsburgh Pirates.

THE BRONX ZOO

Reggie Jackson collected 11 hits during the 1977 postseason, and five of them were home runs.

The 1977 season brought another big free agent to New York. Reggie Jackson had been one of the best sluggers in baseball for a decade, and he knew it. The brash Jackson told reporters, "I didn't come to New York to be a star. I brought my star with me."

Jackson wasn't the only ego on the team. Munson was the team's businesslike captain. He didn't always agree with

Jackson's flashy style. The fiery Martin feuded with his players and Steinbrenner. The dysfunctional team was dubbed "the Bronx Zoo" by pitcher Sparky Lyle.

Despite that, the Yankees reached the 1977 World Series. There, Jackson showed the clutch hitting that earned him the nickname "Mr. October." He hit a two-run homer in the fourth inning of Game 6 against the Los Angeles Dodgers. On his next swing, in the fifth, Jackson added a solo shot. He came up again in the eighth. Once again, he took the first pitch out of the ballpark. The three home runs in one World Series game had been accomplished only once before, by Babe Ruth. And the 8–4 victory clinched New York's first championship since 1962. The Yankees won again the next year, again beating the Dodgers 4–2.

THE CORE FOUR

Steinbrenner's intense style eventually took its toll. He became obsessed with signing big stars, and the team's lineup was always changing. Young prospects were almost

Don Mattingly was a nine-time Gold Glove Award winner for his efforts at first base for the Yankees.

always traded away before they got to New York. After losing the AL Championship Series (ALCS) in 1980 and the World Series in 1981, the Yankees missed the playoffs for the rest of the 1980s. Fans had to settle for cheering on homegrown MVP Don Mattingly, the team's beloved first baseman.

In 1990 controversy caught up with Steinbrenner. It was discovered that he had paid a man to dig up negative information on one of his key players, Dave Winfield. As a result, Steinbrenner was banned from baseball for life. But he returned in 1993 after commissioner Fay Vincent overturned the punishment.

The suspension turned out to be a good thing. It freed general manager Gene Michael to build up the Yankees' roster without his young players being traded. The result was a group of rookies like pitchers Andy Pettitte and Mariano Rivera, catcher Jorge Posada, and shortstop Derek Jeter. The quartet all debuted in 1995 and became known as the "Core Four" as the Yankees returned to contention.

CHAMPIONS AGAIN

The 1996 Yankees had other key pieces like outfielders Bernie Williams and Paul O'Neill. First baseman Tino Martinez had the tough job of replacing the recently retired Mattingly. Martinez won fans over with a team-high 117 RBIs.

That year the team also had a new manager. Joe Torre had not been successful managing other teams, but he fit with the Yankees. Torre never let the pressure of working for Steinbrenner or pleasing the Yankees' demanding fans dent his calm demeanor. That year he led New York back to the World Series.

New York faced the defending champion Atlanta Braves, the best team of the 1990s to that point. Atlanta dominated the first two games, but New York fought back. A dramatic

Pitcher Mariano Rivera is baseball's all-time career leader in saves with 652.

three-run homer by backup catcher Jim Leyritz tied the game 6–6 in the eighth inning of Game 4. The Yankees eventually won in 10 innings to even the series. After a 1–0 shutout in

Game 5, New York returned home with a chance to take the series. A 3–2 win in Game 6 clinched the team's 23rd title.

UNBEATABLE

Two years later the Yankees fielded one of the greatest teams in baseball history. The 1998 lineup set a then-AL record with 114 wins. The team had 10 players with at least 47 RBIs. Five starting pitchers, including newly signed Orlando Hernández, won at least 12 games. Rivera was now one of baseball's dominant closers. His signature pitch, a cut fastball, rode away from right-handed hitters and in on lefties. Everyone struggled to hit it.

Jeter was the centerpiece of the team. Like Mickey Mantle, he had become the idol of New York baseball fans. He was a talented shortstop and an elite hitter, but his good looks and charming personality made him a star off the field too.

The Yankees rolled into the World Series. Their opponents were the San Diego Padres, who were completely overmatched. The Yankees won in a sweep.

The next year New York added even more firepower. Roger Clemens, the reigning Cy Young Award winner as the best pitcher in the league, joined the pitching staff. New York once again cruised to a title. The Yankees won 98 games and then swept the Braves in the World Series.

The 2000 season brought the Yankees' fourth title in five years. This one came with a twist. Many of the team's championships in the 1940s and 1950s came over their New York rivals, the Dodgers and the Giants. But both teams moved to California in the late 1950s. Their replacement was the New York Mets, and in 2000 the Yankees and Mets met in a "Subway Series." The Yankees' streak of 14 consecutive World Series game wins came to an end when the Mets took Game 3. But the Yankees continued their dynasty by winning the series 4–1.

The 9/11 attacks delayed the baseball season so much that the 2001 World Series went later than it ever had before. Game 4 started on Halloween, but the extra-inning game finished after midnight. Derek Jeter eventually won it on a walk-off home run. It was the first run ever scored in the month of November. Though the Yankees eventually lost the series in seven games, Jeter earned the nickname "Mr. November" for his historic homer.

NUMBER 27

It took New York nine years to win the World Series again. In 2009 they had an old roster. Jeter was now 35. Pettitte was 37, Posada was 38, and Rivera was 39. The team also had Alex Rodriguez, Hideki Matsui, and Johnny Damon in the starting lineup. They ranged in age from 33 to 35.

General manager Brian Cashman made some deals to bring in younger stars and give

Designated hitter Hideki Matsui smashes a two-run homer during Game 6 of the 2009 World Series.

the Core Four one last run at a title. The result was New York's best regular season in seven years. The Yankees finished 103–59 and cruised back to the World Series.

It was another banner moment for the Core Four. In a six-game victory over the Philadelphia Phillies, Pettitte won two games. Rivera had two saves, Posada drove in five runs, and Jeter hit .407. But Matsui was the star of the show. In Game 6, the designated hitter drove in six runs in the clinching 7–3 victory. That tied a World Series record for most RBIs in one game previously set by Yankees second baseman Bobby Richardson in 1960. New York took home its 27th championship, the most of any American professional sports team.

HERE COMES THE JUDGE

Over the next five years, the Core Four all moved on. Jeter lasted the longest, retiring in 2014. Yankees fans now looked for the next legend. Thankfully they had a towering figure just about to emerge from the farm system.

At 6 feet, 7 inches and 280 pounds, outfielder Aaron Judge had the size to fill big shoes. And he exploded onto the MLB scene in 2017. Judge set a then-MLB rookie record with 52 home runs. He easily won AL Rookie of the Year honors and finished second in MVP voting.

Injuries held Judge back from building on that promise for the next three seasons. But in 2021, he was back with a 39-homer season to join the MVP conversation again. He was

In addition to his 62 home runs in 2022, Judge led the AL with 131 RBIs and finished second with a .311 batting average.

even better in 2022. Roger Maris's former MLB record of 61 home runs had already been broken, but it was still the AL mark. Judge topped it by hitting his 62nd on October 4. The Yankees won the AL East, but fell short of the World Series. Still, New York fans hoped Judge was the next Yankee legend ready to lead the club back to glory.

TIMELINE

1903

The New York Highlanders join the AL for its third season.

1913

The Highlanders change their name to the New York Yankees.

1919

The Yankees make plans to purchase slugger Babe Ruth from the rival Boston Red Sox in December, making it official in January 1920.

1923

Yankee Stadium opens, and the Yankees win their first World Series.

1927

Ruth and Lou Gehrig star in the "Murderers' Row" lineup that wins 110 games and New York's second World Series title.

1932

Ruth's famous "called shot" home run is the key moment in New York's 4–0 World Series win over the Chicago Cubs.

1941

Joe DiMaggio sets an MLB record by hitting safely in 56 straight games, and the Yankees win their fifth World Series title in six years.

1953

The Yankees win their fifth consecutive World Series title, the longest streak in MLB history.

1956

Don Larsen pitches the first postseason no-hitter as the Yankees capture another title. Larsen's performance still stands as the only postseason perfect game in baseball history.

1961

Roger Maris hits 61 home runs, breaking the record of 60 set by Ruth in 1927.

1977

Reggie Jackson hits three home runs on three consecutive swings in Game 6 of the World Series as the Yankees defeat the Los Angeles Dodgers.

1996

New York wins its first World Series title since 1978.

2000

The Yankees defeat the crosstown New York Mets in the first "Subway Series" since 1956. It is the Yankees third World Series victory in a row.

2009

Designated hitter Hideki Matsui ties a World Series record with six RBIs in the clinching game as the Yankees defeat the Philadelphia Phillies for their 27th championship.

2014

Derek Jeter retires at the end of the season after 20 years with the Yankees.

2017

Outfielder Aaron Judge sets an MLB rookie record with 52 home runs.

2022

Judge hits 62 home runs, passing Maris to establish a new AL record.

TEAM FACTS

FRANCHISE HISTORY

New York Highlanders
(1903–1912)
New York Yankees (1913–)

WORLD SERIES CHAMPIONSHIPS

1923, 1927, 1928, 1932, 1936,
1937, 1938, 1939, 1941, 1943,
1947, 1949, 1950, 1951, 1952,
1953, 1956, 1958, 1961, 1962,
1977, 1978, 1996, 1998, 1999,
2000, 2009

KEY PLAYERS

Yogi Berra (1946–63)
Bill Dickey (1928–43, 1946)
Joe DiMaggio (1936–42,
1946–51)
Whitey Ford (1950, 1953–67)
Lou Gehrig (1923–39)
Reggie Jackson (1977–81)
Derek Jeter (1995–2014)
Aaron Judge (2016–)
Mickey Mantle (1951–68)
Don Mattingly (1982–95)
Thurman Munson (1969–79)
Andy Pettitte (1995–2003,
2007–10, 2012–13)
Jorge Posada (1995–2011)
Mariano Rivera (1995–2013)
Red Ruffing (1930–42,
1945–46)
Babe Ruth (1920–34)
Bernie Williams (1991–2006)

KEY MANAGERS

Miller Huggins (1918–29)
Joe McCarthy (1931–46)
Casey Stengel (1949–60)
Joe Torre (1996–2007)

HOME STADIUMS

Hilltop Park (1903–1912)
Polo Grounds (1912–1922)
Yankee Stadium I (1923–73,
1976–2008)
Shea Stadium (1974–75)
Yankee Stadium II (2009–)

THE SULTAN OF SWAT

Babe Ruth hit 659 of his 714 career home runs in a Yankees uniform. But he actually hit his first career home run against his future team. Ruth's first homer came on May 6, 1915, for the Boston Red Sox against New York.

MONUMENTAL PLAYERS

In 1932 the Yankees created a monument to longtime manager Miller Huggins in center field at Yankee Stadium. In the 1940s, monuments for Babe Ruth and Lou Gehrig were added. When the stadium was renovated in 1976, the three monuments were moved out of the field of play beyond the fence. Today, "Monument Park" includes plaques for several other Yankees greats, including Joe DiMaggio, Mickey Mantle, Yogi Berra, and many others.

THE WISDOM OF AGE

Legendary Yankees manager Casey Stengel was fired by the team after the 1960 World Series. One of the reasons given by the team was that the 70-year-old Stengel was too old. In response, Stengel said, "I'll never make the mistake of being 70 again."

TORRE'S LONG WAIT

Before becoming New York's manager, Joe Torre had played 2,209 MLB games and managed 1,901 more without ever appearing in a World Series. After joining the Yankees, Torre reached the Fall Classic six times in the next eight years.

GLOSSARY

closer

A pitcher who comes in at the end of the game to secure a win for his team.

clutch

An important or pressure-packed situation; a player who often succeeds in important or pressure-packed situations.

colonel

A military rank below general and above major.

dynasty

A team that has an extended period of success, usually winning multiple championships in the process.

farm system

In baseball, all the minor league teams that feed players to one major league team.

free agent

A player whose rights are not owned by any team.

idol

In sports, an athlete who is admired by many fans.

perfect game

A complete game in which a team retires every opposing batter and allows no base runners.

save

When a relief pitcher comes in to finish a close game and secures a win.

shutout

A complete game in which a team allows no runs.

walk-off

Any victory in which the home team scores the winning run in the bottom of the final inning.

MORE INFORMATION

BOOKS

Flynn, Brendan. *The MLB Encyclopedia*. Minneapolis, MN: Abdo Publishing, 2022.

Hewson, Anthony K. *GOATs of Baseball*. Minneapolis, MN: Abdo Publishing, 2022.

Mitchell, Bo. *Ultimate MLB Road Trip*. Minneapolis, MN: Abdo Publishing, 2019.

ONLINE RESOURCES

To learn more about the New York Yankees, please visit **abdobooklinks.com** or scan this QR code. These links are routinely monitored and updated to provide the most current information available.

INDEX

Bauer, Hank, 22, 26

Berra, Yogi, 17, 24, 26, 29

Cashman, Brian, 38

Chambliss, Chris, 32

Chesbro, Jack, 8

Clemens, Roger, 37

Combs, Earle, 14–15

Damon, Johnny, 38

DiMaggio, Joe, 17, 19, 21, 23, 25

Dugan, Joe, 14

Ford, Whitey, 23, 26, 29

Gehrig, Lou, 14–15, 17–19

Gomez, Lefty, 17

Henrich, Tommy, 22

Hernández, Orlando, 37

Huggins, Miller, 13

Hunter, Catfish, 32

Jackson, Reggie, 32–33

Jeter, Derek, 5–7, 35, 37, 38, 40

Judge, Aaron, 40–41

Larsen, Don, 26

Lazzeri, Tony, 15

Leyritz, Jim, 36

Mantle, Mickey, 25–26, 28–29, 37

Maris, Roger, 28–29, 41

Martin, Billy, 22, 32–33

Martinez, Tino, 7, 35

Matsui, Hideki, 38, 40

Mattingly, Don, 34–35

Meusel, Bob, 14

Michael, Gene, 35

Munson, Thurman, 32, 33

O'Neill, Paul, 35

Pettitte, Andy, 7, 35, 38, 40

Pipp, Wally, 14

Posada, Jorge, 7, 35, 38, 40

Randolph, Willie, 32

Reynolds, Allie, 22

Richardson, Bobby, 40

Rivera, Mariano, 7, 35, 37–38, 40

Rizzuto, Phil, 22

Rodriguez, Alex, 38

Ruffing, Red, 17

Ruppert, Jacob, 9, 10

Ruth, Babe, 9–11, 13–17, 27, 33

Steinbrenner, George, 31–35

Stengel, Casey, 24

Torre, Joe, 35

Williams, Bernie, 7, 35

Winfield, Dave, 34

ABOUT THE AUTHOR

Anthony K. Hewson is a freelance writer originally from San Diego. He and his wife now live in the San Francisco Bay Area with their two dogs